Season of Mercy

ALSO BY SALLY ITO

Frogs in the Rain Barrel (poetry, Nightwood Editions, 1995)
Floating Shore (short stories, Mercury Press, 1998)

SEASON
of
MERCY

SALLY ITO

NIGHTWOOD EDITIONS

Published by
NIGHTWOOD EDITIONS
RR #22, 3692 Beach Avenue
Roberts Creek, BC Canada
V0N 2W2

THE CANADA COUNCIL | LE CONSEIL DES ARTS
FOR THE ARTS | DU CANADA
SINCE 1957 | DEPUIS 1957

Cover illustration and design by Kim LaFave
Inside illustrations © 1999 by Akko Nishimura
Author photograph by Paul Dyck
Printed and bound in Canada

Nightwood Editions acknowledges the financial support of
the Government of Canada through the Canada Council for
the Arts for its publishing activities.

Canadian Cataloguing in Publication Data

Ito, Sally, 1964–
    Season of mercy

    Poems.
    ISBN 0-88971-168-2

    I. Title.
PS8567.T63S42 1999   C811'.54   C99-910908-1
PR9199.3.I84S42 1999

This book is dedicated to my husband,
Paul Dyck,
with whom my journey of faith continues.

While you are alive you have a season of mercy . . .
— *Catherine of Siena*

Contents

I.

Crows	11
Of Love and Its Passing	12
To Sin	13
To Adam, the First Poet	14
Temptation	15
Adultery	16
Orbs	17
Hatred	18
Palestine	19
Salt	20
Good Friday	21
The Breath of Giants	22
At the Reynolds Museum Wetaskiwin, Alberta	23
Obituary	24

II.

Madame Blavatsky	27
Esoterica	29
The Cherubs of Cathedral Madeleine	30
Jambudvidpa	31
The Underground Fishermen	32
Rape by Water	33
Tornado	34
What an Old Nisei Artist Told Me	35
La Arribada	36
Caduceus	37
Interpreter	38
The Chastening	39

III.

A Season of Mercy   43
Nazareth   44
Philip and the Ethiopian   45
Constellations   46
The Converted   47
Ash Wednesday   48
The Poor   49
Faith   50
Fumi-e   51
Hikari   52
A Theologian's Hands   53
The Art of Prayer   54
Stone Splendour   56
Mother Tongue   57
Sunday   58

IV.

Myth-maker   61
Words of Advice to the Artist   62
Seahorse   63
Chanson   64
Haecceitas   65
Sao la   66
A Meditation on Semantics   67
The Allure of the Floating Islands   68

Acknowledgements   71

I.

CROWS

Crows have taken away everything –

now *this* and *that*

security
and every kind of
promise that is forever.

Someone said silence is black;

surely *it* was the one that
wrenched the gem from my hand

flapping soundlessly away

into the far corners of the eye,
where light becomes sorrow
and flows endlessly
without words.

OF LOVE AND ITS PASSING

Like turning to the dew in mid-afternoon
and not finding it there . . .

moisture –
damp and stringent,
a feature of that time
has now suddenly grown scaled and dry.

Wooden, they say you become

which is what trees still are,
despite tossing seas,
shifting sandbars, rocky beaches.

Branches that have split skies
can still grow dusky with leaves,
still want to create perfect shadows,

so dew,
dew may linger yet
a little longer.

To Sin

Of the snakes that already reside there,
leave them for they have earned their place;

but of those who have come from outside,
do battle.
Pick up the shield of the serpent-haired
and with it, forest the heart quickly.

Invasions are swift.
Arrows embed deeply
in soft and ponderous places
where hardship has not yet been.

For what innocent yearning exposes
is mighty in its Fall:

a tree shuddering
with fruit.

TO ADAM, THE FIRST POET

God gave you a gift
and with it He said *Name the world*
and so you did,
you, whose once dusty mists
are now the voice
of the dumb beast,
the shuddering branch,
the crashing wave.

Collect and pool the words into song,
rim the eye with the salt of wonder
so sight may utter the speech of the living

and like the soundless urge
that wells in the bird's breast before
the first burst of light on the horizon

your breath is filled
with the inescapable charm of His command,
the babble of His perfection,
wettening the lip with the spittle of forced joy.

Labelling the stars was never your choice,
you said in mute rebellion,
nor rhyming the sea
nor naming the fruit
in whose hand
you first experienced such limits as grief,
named grief,
the sound of your lament
the only original
in all of creation.

TEMPTATION

He who leads me away from prayer
leads me to love you,

you in whom all sighs are wrapped
delicate throbbings of pain
pressing busily on eyes and lips,
proclaiming love like an endless shower of the benign,

when it is more frightfully brutal than that –
this Real Love –
who severs at the knees in one fell swoop
and gathers to its breast
the silent praise of arrows.

ADULTERY

There is some innocence in this transgression
as if in mining the field, the only intent is to plant bulbs,
flower bulbs – bright, exploding stars of ecstasy –
momentary, fragmentary
and of the season only . . .

but the thistles, the small spikes
that enter the flesh after that lethal step
remind too soon, the brittle consequence:

how the heart, tender and wanting
can suddenly burst
like a star
and trail in the sky
the wound of its own shattered light.

ORBS

How with words
we dress one another
destroy ourselves.

How with such succinct brevity,
knife-shaped breath
can wound.

How two plates
crack and create chasms.

Is this what words are for?

Silver discs, blue stones
the hurling voice
the splattering truth
blood-like on faces
sinking into the buried heart
of hearing eyes

that paint only wordlessly
precious

oh, oh, ohs

round, glistening orbs
of true meaning.

HATRED

Behind every hatred
is blindness
so white
that the eye
is but a hissing stream
of opaque fluid.

Throw down your head
hold out your hands
and cup in them
the worst of your fears.

Stare at the dense reflection.

Your face, eyeless.

PALESTINE

Of all landscapes
Palestine seems clearest now
the wind and sand,
desert seas,

the people belonging
and not   but to some
other God, they call
Jahweh not Allah

and the constant
bitter sand-spittle
of words, words, words
that takes lives, hostages,
shoots and kills.

The inner din of this
battle has been a dull throb
between the ears

so much

the yearning becomes
the clamour for a messiah to redeem
from this small strip of land

peace and the sound of water.

SALT

Suddenly salt has lost its savour.

Love and all that it meant
is now a fragment of a bowl
no longer capable of holding water
but of only this caked white reflection –

a self, distorted and wan,

weary with lines of knowing,
scarred with wounds that have truly savoured,
and known no other cleansing.

GOOD FRIDAY

The dark, hard suffering in our bones
does not always reveal faith.

The eye whose centre is washed
perpetually by tears
can only know the constant
measure of its liquid shape

and no more.

Perhaps *this* is the failure of us all –
such weak, vinegared despair
sponged onto the gaping hole of our *I thirst*

This wine before death
is always blood.

THE BREATH OF GIANTS

There is nothing so unpleasant
as the breath of giants
down your back,

so a crazy man told me,

a man who once had visions of the Golden City,
Kingdom of God, Utopia
and the Triumphant World
of the Proletariat . . .

One step,
and   SPLAT,
that's the end

he said

like, you know,
the Friendly Giant
gone berserk?

All those little farmhouses,
trees and fences, children laughing

Finished.

Gritting his teeth,
he ground his fist
into the palm of his hand.

Such hands
I took into mine,
pressed warm and tight,
like two trembling doves

wishing for them,
a silent piercing
a quiet releasing.

AT THE REYNOLDS MUSEUM
WETASKIWIN, ALBERTA

Beyond the museum of the automobile
and the Aviation Hall of Fame
is a wide field filled with the rusted, hulking frames
of yesterday's machines.

Between the orderly rows of rotting red
are speckles of sheep
blithely grazing
under the rickety spout
of some old combine
or beside the shell
of an old beast
that roared down highways
belching smoke and steam.

When all our remembering and finger-pointing
is done at the museum,
we can sit outside and watch the sheep
minister to the noble folly of this –
our clunking, rusted age.

Obituary

Someone has died today.
The circle of their truth
has closed,
shuttered out the light.

Meanwhile, we still go on
as if the sound of our breathing
will issue warrants,
the reasons for living.

Our hour,   *you see*
has not yet come

We scan the pages
briefly read the moments of a life
whose time *has* come –

small, measured words
must mark the most
significant moment of all –

our passing into silence.

II.

MADAME BLAVATSKY

The definition of theosophy,
of which she could be called the founding mother, is:
*Any speculative system basing knowledge of nature
on intuitional or traditional knowledge of God.*

The key word is
intuitional.

Roll it a bit
on the tongue,
see if it comes out
amorphously,
like clouds of breath
on a cold night.

Traditional is more easy.
It is Ann Landers logic –
precise bits of glass
that are neither jar nor bottle,
but suitable for mirrors –
big, small, weighty, thin.

Madame Blavatsky
was the kind of woman
men got involved with,
poets like Yeats
who was waiting, pining,
for the big bang –
night's exploding consciousness
on his sun dripping days.

They don't know *intuition, tradition;*
they know only silver trumpets,
and the riding of horses in broad daylight.

They don't know night
like Madame Blavatsky does,
how she wraps it around her waist like an apron,

rolls up her sleeves,
and washes, washes
everything in its waters.

ESOTERICA

It is the inevitable decline into detail,
the curve of a gabled temple roof
once signifying the god's jewelled touch
now becoming an oracle
of the copulating word,
the twisting of memory.

When empires collapse,
it is said their universities
telegraph the event
by swelling into watery knots
of stippled decay
forming blemishes
on the corpse to be.

Esoterica

This knowledge
of the finely microscopic,
this bellows of the bloated word
fanning with ardour
a perfect hollow of air
is its own beautiful decoration
and like art for art's sake,
is a mask of clever detail
behind which hearts may hide,
the mind sinking in pleasure before
the thunder of hooves,
the looming chariot,
the dark storm of doubt.

THE CHERUBS OF CATHEDRAL MADELEINE

They were for sale,
little wooden cherubs
wings stiff against each other
in square boxes in the
back corner of the cathedral.

Holding one for a moment,
I thought it a fanciful souvenir
from a cathedral in Paris –
just what would perfectly adorn
a plain wooden door at home.

They were sold by a faceless woman –
any woman in the darkness
that is peddling is not a face
but a mere whirl of swift exchanging hands.

I bought one, or two,
I can't remember.

Later I read about Jesus in the temple
sweeping away the seller's wares
his hand dashing against those wooden objects
setting them free,
winged and away from their boxes
to taste at last,
the bright white air.

JAMBUDVIDPA
The Everyday Human Realm

So flat and slick this circle
of everydayness,
it is hard to perceive the centre axis,
the pole of ascending heavens
and descending hells
each a circular realm
unto itself.

Like many stacked coins
of various sizes,
this cosmology
of which we are only
a faint, barely discernible part
vibrates,
a seething hive of truth,
into which hands plunge
and are stung
again and again.

This is the circle of repeating life
it says,
death and rebirth.

Hands recoil once more
into jambudvidpa,
our blissful ignorance,
realm of the everyday.

The Underground Fishermen

They lie beneath the
ceilings of our eyelids
in a dark and damp grotto.

There is a pool of black water
into which they cast their lines
from the dusky shore –

many lines crossing
like webs, silver strings dancing
across the inky surface.

Their faces are dark and penetrating
as scholars brooding over obscure texts.

Leviathan creeps along those waters,
is the *Big One* of their dreams,
the one that got away,
the one they've come to fish for again, and again,
in this dusky, dim grotto
concealed under our sleeping lids.

RAPE BY WATER

Woman
having been shoved into it
cold and eddying around the calves,
is forced to bow down
squat at the knees.

The urn shaped air between her legs
disintegrates like decaying clay
into the muddying, fish-filled waters
as she screams *OH NO OH NO*

Water is not a lover
it will not caress the face
nor the small part of the ear
that feels the exquisite moisture of
another's breath.

Water does not eat words,
will not fatten nor bloat
on sad paragraphs of wilted sunlight;

Love is a foreign notion
quickly swallowed like a stone
by muddy beds tracked by amphibians
whose small broad leaps into the air
engender conception
from the protesting *o's*
of a woman's darker mouth.

TORNADO

In a dream,
there was a field
with great white tornadoes
circling above the dark earth.

Something more powerful
than a hundred tractors tilled that field,
haloes of circled blades
digging into the soil.

The force of wind was
tremendous, violent
but it had done more
than the hand of man
ever could.

God spoke to Job
from a whirlwind
and asked,

Who endowed the heart with wisdom
or gave understanding to the mind?

It must have been overwhelming;
how did he bear it,   Job,
his body pelted with words –
God's hard seed?

WHAT AN OLD NISEI ARTIST TOLD ME

plant circles
she said
cover them with soil
and let old wounds
become trees

that is how i did it
she said

burning circles on paper
until even
neglecting her children,
she found herself

on that brink,
turning suddenly
to step quite certainly
on the broad path
her hands had etched
so painstakingly.

i remember
the most naturally drawn of them,
– the circles –
a tree ring,
stone-brown.

after the broad blasting shout of colour
she must have found what
was most peaceful

herself,
the core,
a dropped stone
that leaves
no ripple.

LA ARRIBADA*

They have arrived,
    the slow finned creatures
out of darkness, wading
then clambering up onto the sand
to lay their eggs.

    In dreams
they are harbingers of a slower time, a more graceful time
    through thick blue, viscous green;
a pod of sea notes
    rising gently to the surface
hitting the high note of a life
spent entirely in water.

    If all our lives,
we were waiting   like them
for the time to birth our children,

would we seem less anxious

if we glanced back at the bruised womb of the sea
from whence we too, were born?

    See her open mouth
sigh at the small wonder of our departing hearts
    throbbing to give life
        to the precious ache
of her containment.

* The name given for the mass arrival of ridley sea turtles on shore
to hatch their eggs.

CADUCEUS

It is winged and narrow,
made out of gold,
stiff as an arrow.

It is Hermes' privileged wand

and the broad, muscled arm
that holds it

is a priest's.

o angry

that i am against its power,
i, the impotent book-hurler, at
its relentless *truth, truth, truth*

whose swift pointed song,
the gift of the dove,

wounds suddenly.

INTERPRETER

I am afraid to read
just as I am afraid of being murdered.

It's become so bad
that every book I pick up is a murder weapon –
blue-edged knives,
delicate, aromatic poisons,
clever handcrafted pistols,
and a range of other bizarre killing oddities –
ninja stars, batons,
brass knuckles.

Words have a way at getting at the body;
every book in your hand
is an opportunity for suicide,
self-obliteration.

When I was a child,
I promised myself
I would put the Bible in my teeth,
roll up my sleeves, and roar,
roar with the might of lions.

Now it seems,
I'd much rather walk blindfolded,
backward into their jaws,
      wait like Daniel,
unarmed, faithful
interpreter of dreams.

And if I cannot read
for the life in me,
I can at least dream.

Dreaming is an art.
Dreaming is wise;
its parchment, water
its words, the blue ink of a
nightingale's song.

THE CHASTENING

It is nearly over:
this lesson
in which you
have whipped me
ten times
with saplings
dusted with snow,
blossoms, leaves.

The wise croaking
of frogs could have
not taught me more
than your hand
passing against my head.

The wind is strong
ardent with your words:

Chasten, chastening

In me you have dwelled
taken the blood in my fingers
and etched fanciful
designs on my palms.

You have given
my heart to birds
and have told me
many times:

Stand alone.

Gazing through the dark window,
I have seen,
even through my schoolgirl tears,

a delicious spring,
blue flights of fancy,

a switch with a sprig of green.

III.

A Season of Mercy

A season of mercy
has been granted us,
this long time now –
          history
     by crucifixion
has always demanded patience.

House after house
has been built on the shore,
the same fishermen fishing seas
for the One man who spoke to them
from on the water.

Some are tired of waiting;
some have lain down to die,

but still others persist
with dew on their eyes
so that even I must turn
this long time now
to face Him   at last
mercy's desire
granted.

NAZARETH

The road that winds from it,
is just as narrow
as that man said it was,

the carpenter's son
who must have travelled it,

stepping out into the wide
expanse of desert and hills,
to set on his brow,
the crown of time's circling
days and nights.

Oh, suffering!
the pain of knowing,

and then,
having to wait,

wait endlessly.

PHILIP AND THE ETHIOPIAN

We are all like that eunuch
sitting in a chariot,
reading difficult texts,
wondering what meaning is,

when it seems that it has always
been running after us,
clouded only by the dust
of our racing wheels.

The man in the distance
keeping pace
has always been there;
will always know the secret meaning
of all the sacred passages;
will know where water is,
and where to baptize.

But let us stop the chariot,
and ask ourselves this,
How can we truly know?
and see,   at last,
this limping, panting
messenger of Love.

CONSTELLATIONS

. . ultimately, and precisely in the deepest and most
important matters, we are unspeakably alone; and many
things must happen, many things must go right, a whole
constellation of events must be fulfilled, for one human
being to successfully advise or help another.
                    – Rainer Maria Rilke, *Letters to a Young Poet*

After the getting of our destinies,
it seems there could have been no other way.

All the hurts, denials, betrayals –

yes, every one of them

accountable,
accounted for

as each star in the darkness is.

A long battle of constellations we are,
clinging clandestinely
to light after light
swinging back into darkness,
once more into mercy.

THE CONVERTED

For those
whose moment it is not,
the eyes of those for whom it is
appear dew infested, their convictions
questionable as a carcass eroded by light.

Secretly pining after their indignity,
we wonder where such wholesale slaughter has occurred.

Where in the mind
did the self lay down and die?

The morning's water on the eye
of those who attend
to the moment
is the smallest of resurrections
before the great dawning of light,
the promise of heaven
on darkness entombed.

ASH WEDNESDAY

Now then,
let us put on the spirit of our weakness,
bow down before the glory of our shame,
remember the dust
out of which the crown of thorns
took root, bore fruit
from the seeds of our fallen hearts.

There is triumph in our brokenness,
bread in our suffering.

The cross of ashes
is the mud of earth,
the black wound
of our deliverance.

THE POOR

all that they asked was that we should continue to
remember the poor . . .

– Galatians 2:10

Without their nourishment,
where would we be?

Bloated without sense,
raw pouches of watery wealth,
wind-pockets of words
sandbags of security, a sleeping inertia
shored up, shored up, shored up
against some tide that will never come.

The poor are always with us . . .

as if they had never been,
as if our eyes had been fixed only on the sky.

Where are they who are our mirrors
sleeping in the small shade of our luxuries,
the sand in our satin?

When we look at them without flinching
into the dark holes of their eyes

continuous, eternal, wanting, weary

we look into our souls' smallest oasis
– the deepest wells of our hidden repentance.

FAITH

Faith
is a stone
in the belly

– a kind of
jonah that
must take
account of
its empty
surroundings

sitting,
meditating.

It is a round, grey
medium of certainty
that acts as breaker,
cornerstone.

So simple is its substance,
yet so dense with weight

no one yet
has sought to create it
out of lesser things

much less wish for it
with eyes that squint and marvel
at its longsuffering.

No, it is a given thing
warmed in the palms of He
who knew most intimately

of what the Kingdom is made.

FUMI-E*

They were heretics of a sort,
refusing to step on the fumi-e,
martyred on stakes in the sea
where the tide consumed
their last full sigh of life.

What possessed these simple fishermen and their families
to worship the coveted icons –
a star of David, a wooden cross, statues of Mary,

hide them in their
crudely converted altars of Buddha
at the price of death

is as much a mystery as prayer itself.

As fire consumes
so does water,

the very stroke of death,
the very breath of faith.

* The fumi-e was a flat stone or metal plate, etched with the
picture of Christ. The Tokugawa Shogunate used the fumi-e to
expose Christians. Belief in Christianity had been made illegal by
the Shogunate. Anyone who could not step on the fumi-e was
deemed a traitor to the nation and was either tortured or put to
death.

HIKARI

After Seeing a documentary on
Kenzaburo Oe, Nobel Laureate, 1996

He named his son 'Light' –
Hikari, the word is in Japanese –
and the son, his dark eyes slightly askew
was diagnosed mentally handicapped.

The father who was a writer
was greatly troubled, disturbed
by a pair of eyes so opaque
they never shed tears
even when the hands
chopped onions.

At Hiroshima, he floated a lantern of the dead
for the still living boy.
HIKARI said the lamp,
sailing down the river
with all the other dozens of dead
whose light was snuffed out
by that obscene parody of
the sun exploding . . .

Books were written about Hikari,
books on the torment and delight of handicap,
books that longed to console the heart of a suffering parent.

Now thirty, the boy who still cannot shave himself
composes music, his simple mind now a dance of notes,
so particular and fine,
they grace the writer's brow
with laurel so sweet, words melt into bliss,
and are forever kept
from the edge of the mouth's last precipice –
the uttering of   Despair,
which now, at last,
is in the season of its shame.

A Theologian's Hands

are as rough as the hands
that formed them,

weighty tomes of just shed dust
now fingering
the remote possibility
of returning
to that once state
when all certainty
was only one hand contemplating
the whole universe.

Now many are the hands that
attempt to make memory
out of that which formed them

pen myths of understanding
for a word-bound creation

myths about hands so clever
the earth died in them
for them.

Word after word
fist over fist
ideas in flesh

so that all hands may feel
the hard clasp of the other
in holy prayer.

THE ART OF PRAYER
to Paul

When you pray
    take two stones
and breathe on them.

One stone for yourself.
One stone for another.

To the first stone
       make complaint
Rest it on a bed of thorns
Tell it your shortcomings
Turn it left and right
making sure all is
thoroughly pierced,
purged.

To the second stone,
       kiss the surface
so that it will be warmed.
Pay close attention to
the grooves and holes
and speckled surfaces
for there is no
other stone like it
in the world.
Hold it in your hand,
carry it in your pocket
remember   always   to bring it out
into the light.

When you have learned to hold
these two stones together,
you will have learned the art of prayer.

Now find two such stones;
        now go
to riverbeds, mountainsides,
    gardens and deserts.

Now go, go alone.

STONE SPLENDOUR

Stone splendour
and the blue distance of words
cleave me in two

(wanting *You*
and not *You*,
the innermost sound of *You*
from which *You* are made)

Give me the sound that
in the stone dwells,
the wordless shape
of breathful blue

together they will be, must be

united

blue stone word
word blue stone
stone blue word

Give me the hearing eyes
to see the touched *You* speak

I will, *You* say

in prayer.

MOTHER TONGUE

. . . the world before
the wound of english

the birth words

    sounds now foreign

and oh, the labour of effort
to return to that soft curve in the tongue

where mother's milk lay.

SUNDAY

Jerusalem
having been walled in this week
now lets its stone openly weep.

Erosion,
dull throbbing prayer,
has had its toll

– the meaningless chisel
of words unmeant

releasing at last
this flood of pebbles,
a dry spittle for eyes to be rubbed with.

This then – knowledge of the ruinous
which eats at the Holy
must suddenly renew itself

in Sunday silence,
with water fresh
from the Rock.

IV.

MYTH-MAKER

Do you remember
what it was to create a world –

to take from the naked
and pillage with clothing
the self?

Creating stories
was to stay awake in them

not sleep nor dream
the shapeless edges
away from them.

Long after the dissolution, the undressing
the small self will be left
        the sparrow
            the pebble
                    the eye
whose circle of fabled knowledge
will grow certain
in the coming light.

WORDS OF ADVICE TO THE ARTIST

In the end
we are defined only
by those who love us,

whose hands have
known the touch of our words,
whether blows, caresses,
slaps or embraces.

They matter to us
only because we do not
respect them
properly   significantly.

We would rather
grow flowers for strangers
than show them the purple bruises
of our open hearts.

Being an artist
is opening the wound
that is in breathing.

Let us not forget then
who has loved us, before
the flowered breath slips
deceitfully out our
bleeding lips.

SEAHORSE

Its delicacy is the poet's;
the concerns   indulgences
emotions
curving into a tight tail
that winds around
the most fragile tendril of seaweed.

The eyes are dumb, mute
and the snout a long hollow tube
from which the music of bubbles
appear   disappear.

This breath is just enough
to bring forth the froth
of some sweltering sea thought

and set into motion
this slim, quivering wisp of a messenger

CHANSON

    When we sing
the small beauty and rage
of the heart

    the hand trembles to touch
the clock that is ticking there

Time
the beat of it in words
is the only human act
    that arrests it   briefly

But a respite   as powerful

as the first storm
    that created the world
that brought forth
the trilling bird
    the singing wave

that shaped from dust
this hollow mouth
into sound.

HAECCEITAS

Suchness,
the way of things
in things

Driving by stubbled fields under a pale blue sky
in the cold clear afternoon of November,
there are dogs   farm dogs
half mangy, black white brown yellow mutts
    ambling in ditches
        sniffing the sky
            chasing speedy nothings
                rolling in the dry grass.

They are in their state.   *Haecceitas.*

Undisturbed in their element
bliss in their blood
undetected but for
    this eye
that passes like sudden flame
to fire their beings
into this quiet art
which is the poet's own private
haecceitas.

SAO LA

There are still mysteries in this world, for example
sao la, delicate deer creature,
one of the few mammals to be discovered this century
emerges from a Vietnamese wood,
is captured and dies.

Are there yet more creatures like you
        at the fringes of the eye
in that unknown dreaming of the universe
that continues on without us:
        Nature pulsing with the breath
our unattending selves?

These that live   go on
remarkably without us

sao la

you call for a revolution beyond the eyes
to seek within the observing outward self

a wonder unseen –
Creation, functioning for itself,
in pleasure only for its God.

A Meditation on Semantics

On a walk
in the snowy afternoon
by a frozen lakeside
the flight of birds,
tufts of yellowed grass,
darkened branches

are not connected

but by the stream of the eye
with its downward brushstroke of
sense   wonder   word.

Hands that touch the smoothest snow
will reach with the same curiosity for a book
to glean too, from its ivory fields
the snowflake's mystery.

The pages are as orderly as the seasons
for in them we have numbered the sun's passage
around the self, have measured its purpose
with songs from the chariot.

Tomorrow in those yet unprinted pages
we can still write of the intricate designs of hope
carved into of the flesh of our palms
even though we will have
no other words
for the darkness we grow into,
the silence that we find
in the stone of the matter:

our certain death.

But that we have given it a name
gives us the comfort of knowing
and that is all that is necessary
to live.

Having settled in
on one green isolation,
it appears there are many more –
a speckle of truths
round and perfect as stones;

nowhere a path
leading
but to the water that separates.

Each has built around itself
a fringe of bright coral
declared itself a
permanent beauty

but should you be foolish
to declare yourself resident,
the truth will thread your
hair with dazzling nests
of ghosts, half resurrects,
the reincarnated
soulless, headless, heartless
beings who invade quickly
you, for whom belief
was once easy
not this twisted labour of
mythic green.

What then
but floating abysses?
not isolations
but the bloom of black tradition
truth's gaping petals
a dense mystery
drawing you down into wholes
that only drown.

if having found truth once
it will find you again,

volcanoes yet are shaped from
what is deep
inside;
doves do dwell there
and can be released
by hands that trust most blindly
for shore

in a once
and still always once
shoreless world.

ACKNOWLEDGEMENTS

I wish to acknowledge the support of Marisa Alps whose
continued interest in my work through her years with
Nightwood has been an inspiration and an encouragement.
Thanks also to Atsuko Nishimura, artist and friend, who has
contributed her artwork to fulfill the vision of my poetry.
Kim LaFave is also to be thanked for his design work on this
book.

Some of the poems have appeared previously in *Another
Way to Dance: Contemporary Asian Poetry from Canada
and the United States*, *Event* magazine and the *Stroll of
Poets Anthology*.